Lilies of the Field

How to Obtain Peace During Difficult Times

DEBBIE VANDERSLICE

WESTBOW
PRESS®
A DIVISION OF THOMAS NELSON
& ZONDERVAN

WestBow Press books may be ordered through booksellers or by contacting:

WestBow Press
A Division of Thomas Nelson & Zondervan
1663 Liberty Drive
Bloomington, IN 47403
www.westbowpress.com
1 (866) 928-1240

ISBN: 978-1-9736-9804-3 (sc)
ISBN: 978-1-9736-9803-6 (e)

Print information available on the last page.

WestBow Press rev. date: 08/03/2020

Contents

Dedication

to hannah banana the world's best daughter. i love you so much
to sherry thank you for your continued support
to leigh ann for your skill
to kay for being my best friend
to cynthia, chip,edy gibbons, mom and
crew for being there always
to the westbow staff for all your patience with me

About the Author

Debbie Vanderslice graduated with honors in history from SMU in Dallas, Texas, where she played tennis on a full scholarship. With her strong writing skills and love for God she has gone on to work with such companies as DaySpring, Celebration, and Warner Press as a freelance writer. In 2008 she had Shameless, a women's indepth bible study published by New Hope Publishers. She has also published Gilead Now by Westbow Publishers, and Treasures of Darkness by Westbow Publishers as well as And the House Was Filled by Westbow as well.

Debbie seeks to minister to hurting women who have gonethrough many trials and tribulations. Debbie has fought many personal battles, including an eating disorderand attends AA. Debbie's passion can be seen in theexample of Jesus commanding others to take of their Lazarus' grave clothes, as she ministers to those tryingto become free from past issues and mistakes. Debbie currently teaches and writes full time.

Debbie was a nationally ranked tennis player who won several state championships, was the eighth ranked amateur in the nation in singles and the third ranked doubles amateur player in the nation. She has coached state champions and has coached on the high school as well as collegiate level. She enjoys reading, running, and spending time with her family. She currently resides in Little Rock, Arkansas, and has one daughter.

Part 1

THE PROBLEM

The Field

1 Corinthians 3:9 "For we are God's fellow workers.
You are God's field. God's building."
(ESV)

Before me was an open field full of Indian paintbrushes. In fact we were with,my best friend and prayer partner, Martha, who had died over a year ago, but was now running to and fro in a shin length white robe and as met me in the lush green field, Martha gave me the biggest hug I had ever had before. I didn't know what to say so I said," Martha, you've got hair." She laughed and said, "But of course." A man in the distance, with auburn hair and a beard, plus a purple robe waited patiently. "Where are you going?" I'm going with the king." I said kind of excitedly, I want to go too?" Martha said, "It's not your time yet." And then she was gone.

I am convinced that I had a near death experience after having a near fatal stroke. I was without a heartbeat for over 2 minutes. Those two minutes changed my life forever.

I have always been skeptical of near death experiences but that changed the day I "died" for two minutes. The only thing I heard that ride in the ambulance was, "she's back. We got her." But that dream was the most vivid dream I have ever had. Needless to say

I am a big believer in near death experiences. I am pretty sure I had one.

I believe all of us are born with a clean slate, then comes life and all the tainting of that slate. We sin, and then there is sin done to us.

As babies we are sinless. After all, babies only eat, sleep, and poop. All day every day. Some Bible scholars say we are born sinners. I find that absurd. It is not until we are at the age of accountability that we are then responsible for our sin. I believe each person is different. Some are accountable at age 10 or 11 and some are 17 or 19. There is no hard and fast rule that a certain age is for all children. It is not for me to say or judge each person and their age of accountability.

I believe all of us are born with a clean slate then as times come life and the tainting of that slate. We sin and then sin is done to us. As babies we are sinless. After all, they only eat, sleep, and Poop. I believe each person and their situation is different. Thus, different ages of accountability. Some are 10 or 11 while others are 17 or 18. There are no hard and fast rules when the age of accountability.

Babies and small children do not know right and wrong. They, like toddlers and small children do not know sin or the consequences of sin. They, as toddlers, learn right verses wrong on their upbringing. But to fathom heaven and the cross, and forgiveness of sins, is mentally and spiritually beyond their capabilities. When are they ready for that? Like I said earlier, each person and child are different. My daughter for example, said at the dinner table when she was only 4 "Come inside me Jesus." And then thanked Him for the pizza we were about to eat. Was it a true confession of Christ? I think so. No she didn't pray the sinners prayer. Just a child like prayer and faith.

We do not come into this world sinful, although some will say we do. No, we are a clean slate much like the 19th century black boards in the schools. Life begins to happen to us. We are like an open freshly cut field. After living in this world we have faced sin done to us and sin we have done to others.

I am not worried at all about my daughter's salvation experience. I t was a child's faith. She has redone it several times, just to make sure. Although she was only four she understood what sin was and who Jesus was, her Savior.

My revival was three words. I said "Jesus come inside." That was it. No angels singing. No earthquake that I know of. No tombs disturbed. Just me going to the restroom. I call it the restroom revival. The impact was immediate. I stopped cheating in school. My friends were shocked. I played better tennis and my grades skyrocked. Things were still the same with my family. But I did change, not the circumstance.

I wonder if this was how Paul felt? In a grimy, rat infested prison cell. No bathroom. No real food. His circumstance did not change, but boy, did he change. In muck and mire he penned most of the New Testament. He was all about Christ. Christ alone. I also like to think that field represents our lives. We are all born with a clean slate or open field. Some scholars say we are born sinners, while others say the age of accountability is around 12 or 13. If we are all sinners at birth while others are older say 6 or 7 then it is up to God to determine His, not man's, age of accountability. Some preachers say that all are sinners, even toddler. I have yet to find a toddler who understood the Gospel when eating his Cherrios. This is the type of Christians who say give your soul to God but send your money to us. This is a slap to God's face. He is not a coke machine. In goes the money(request) and out comes the desired product or answered prayer the way you want life to go. I call this the Coke machine gospel.

What is the problem? The field. While we are all now on an open field or slate, some of us have a field of weeds or whatever is your favorite flower. As life goes on we will have some bad things that happen to us, weeds, or some good things that will Why bad things happen to good people is beyond my scope of understanding. All I know is that good can happen out of bad.

Just keep putting one foot in front of the other. We are all given a different field. And it is up to us to not only live with it, but the thrive with it. After all, it is really God's field, we are merely the tenants of this field.

No atrocity is greater than the 6 million Jews that were murdered during WWII. But it doesn't end there. The survivors were brave beyond belief, and out of something so evil can come Good. The Diary of Anne Frank was one such thing. A peek for WWII came out of her diary. I can think of no stronger race or people than the Jews during that war. Pretty bleak to say the least but good always trumps evil/bad. Especially by a madman named Hitler. We should learn a lesson from them.

The Jewish faith was spurred on and now have more than those who were murdered during the war II

The problem is that peace sort of disappears when we have an uneven field. Just ask the Jews during WWII .They were not given a level playing field. Was it bad? Without a doubt. Did it change lives? Without a doubt. Good always triumphs over bad. Just think of the Cross. Satan thought he had won when Christ conquered death and rose from the grave. He alone is our salvation. He alone is our redemption. He alone is our forgiveness. He alone is our everything.

I have always thought that Christ is the ultimate and the great equalizer. He transcends all races, religions, and societal classes no matter our playing field, no matter how dirty our playing field is, Christ can make it clean again. No one knows this better than Julie Miller. Her song, Broken Things, highlights how Christ makes the playing field even, again and again. As much as we need it. Redemption is not a onetime event. No redemption happens

Over and over. Forgiveness is an ongoing situation. If you experienced abuse then the playing field is stacked. When there is great sin, there is grace a ton more. Out of the abyss, comes greater love. The cross is always bigger and better than Satan's perceived shame. Shame is God's glory. All we need to do is give it to Christ. No matter our playing field. After all, it is God's playing field!!!!!!!!!!!!!!

Road Blocks

1 Corinthians 9:2b
"...but we endure anything rather
than put an obstacle in the way
in the Gospel of Christ."
(ESV)

I was desperate to get there. They needed me. There were orange and white barrels all over one lane. I only had two miles to go before I would reach my friends at that very important place. OTB, On The Border. It was my birthday and I needed to get to the restaurant on time. I was clearly late. Because of the construction I was officially late.

You've been there before. Stuck in traffic because of the almighty construction. Just like you slow down in traffic because of road blocks, so too can you be stalled in a relationship not any with others but yourself and even God. I think we get stuck because of disbelief and anger.

There are many road blocks towards us as we try to obtain peace. I got stuck over fifteen years while mourning my best friend and prayer partner. I t was not until I celebrated Martha's life that I began to heal. Healing is relevant to each individual. I agree with Kubler-Ross stages of grief. Can you get stuck? Absolutely. If someone tells you to move on, just tell them you are...in your own time frame. Not their's. But your's.

Road blocks are not all bad. Actually, they are good. Even the orange and white barrels on your much run in car is good. It means they are working on the road...yeah. These barrels mean slow down or stop. It means slow down, potential danger ahead. They are working for the road ahead. Making it better for you and your family ahead. What did we do before GPS? They are aiding in going around the road block and potential danger.

As much as like to think they are out to get me and want me to be at work, they really are just doing their job and trying to make it better and easier on our driving commutes. What about roads that are not taken?

Even in the midst of pain and suffering a broken road may lead us straight to where we are suppose to be. This song is right on target about a crooked road that leads us straight to the Lord. Look at these verses that turns a roadblock into a highway. Which one is your favorite? Why?

Romans 8:28 "And we know that for those who love God all things work together for good."(ESV)

Genesis 50:20 "As for you, you meant evil against me, but God meant it for good." (ESV)

Philippians 1:6 "I am sure of this, that he who began a good work in you will bring it to completion at the day of Jesus Christ." (ESV)

1Timothy 4:4 "For everything created by God is good and nothing is to be rejected if it is received with thanksgiving..."(ESV)

1Peter 1:3a blessed be the God and Father of our Lord Jesus Christ! According to His great mercy, he

*has caused us to be bornagain to a living hope through
the resurrection of Jesus Christ from the dead."
(ESV)*

Which is your favorite? Why? What is amazing grace. Getting something you don't deserve? Let's look at someone we all know. Oprah Winfrey. Or as we call her, O. Pregnant at age14, poor, no education. Not going anywhere, right? Wrong, wrong, wrong. She now runs a billion dollar industry. How? She is quite humble. By the grace of God, she says time and time again. Millions look to her for inspiration. She is a postcard for living beyond abuse. She endured abuse, physical and sexual, and look at her now. Her chains are gone.

Contentment

Philippians 4:11b
"...for I have learned whatever situation I am to be content..."
(ESV)

Read the following verses and choose your favorite.

Philippians1:21 "For to me to live is
Christ, and to die is gain." (ESV)

Philippians 4:4 "Rejoice in the Lord, again I say rejoice." (ESV)

Philippians 13:4 "For he was crucified in weakness,
but lives but lives by the power of God."(ESV)

There is a difference between being content versus being happy. Happy is a feeling whereas being content is being totally satisfied. You are happy to order shrimp fahitas, but content having eaten them. Paul lived in a dirty floor, chained, no bathroom, or room service. Oh and no heat or air conditioner to stifle the smell.

This is the same man who held the coats of the people who stoned to death Stephen. He despised Christians until that day.

The day God blinded him on the road/way to Damascus. He was blinded by Christ. His come to Jesus meeting just got personal. people used to think, "was this the man who hated Christians so much?

No other believer was on fire as Paul was. He gave it all up, even his life, for Jesus. Would you have gone there with what all Paul did for Christ? Paul was God's chosen instrument. No pressure. It was on the road to Emmaus that his life was changed for ever. Countless Bible studies have been done on this very topic. It is here that Paul heard God's call and direction on his life. The change in Paul's life was immediate.

I was 17 when I heard the call to follow Christ. Where was I? the church? The car? A retreat? Where? In the bathroom!!!!!!!!!! I kid you not. I call it the restroom revival. I said, "come inside me?" that was it. No angels. No blinding light. Just a simple prayer or plea. I immediately stopped cheating in school. My classmates were shocked at my refusal to stop cheating in school. My inward change manifested itself in an outward action. I had the fool proof cheating method in French. On the oral part of the test my friend, who I will not name, would lift her head up from her desk on the right answer only. Pretty good huh? No, when I gave my life to Christ, I stopped cheating in all areas of my life. Honesty was the main component in this change. Christ was inside me now, I wanted to reflect that change. My friend was shocked. In fact, the whole class was shocked.

I believe our circumstances define us. It is all about how we respond TO that circumstance. So either we see the cup as half full or half empty. We can either be positive or negative. One generation or family of origin las a lot to do the this a certain amount. The hymn below was penned by a man who lost all four of his children to an ocean liner that went down. He penned this hymn just days after his children drowned. It think you have probably heard or sung it satisfied or content in all circumstances. It is up to us. We either accept our circumstance or we reject it. When I was about 10 years old I said if I could just be 15 I'll be better. Then at 15 I wanted to be 20 or 21. I am now 50. I no longer want to be older!! What changed? My circumstances changed. It, time, will wait for no one. Situations change. People rarely do.

We can do our own thing, go down the very road we create. Or we can wait until He is invited in to us. Christ is a gentleman, He never goes anywhere He is not invited to. See if you can relate to this poem I wrote. We each have a choice. We have them every day. Fried or scrambled? Walk or the car? Trump or Hilliary? Marriage or divorce? Victor or victim? Heaven or hell. Life or death? And the list just goes on and on.

That Old Dam
By Debbie Vanderslice

Shameless New Hope Publishing 2008 p. 70-71
Gilead Now Westbow Publishers p. 43-44
Tate Publishers p. 56-58

John8:32
"Then you will know the truth, and the truth will se
you free."(ESV)
After years and years the old dam broke.
Many of the townspeople were stunned;
their lives held captive by the overflow of water.
Everyone was caught off guard.
Except for Red.
Red was the little old man who fished everyday at that old dam.
Whether it was 100 degrees in August and he had to
battle the stifling summer heat with no hint of a hot
breeze, or it was a snowy day in December.
his frozen fingers wrapped around is old cane pole,
Red went fishing just the same.
One day a town committee went to Red's home to ask
him questions about that old dam.
"Did you see it comin?"

"Did you know ahead of time? Is that why you stopped fishing?"
"Did you see it coming?"
"We know you didn't know, otherwise you would have
let the town folks know."
Red let them answer their own questions more or less,
and he chuckled with his tongue in cheek.
Yes, he thought to himself, I'd seen it coming. He
had known the dam would one day break,
but he never knew exactly when.
Red didn't merely watch the red and white plastic cork
bob up and down. He'd look around every now and then
while fishing on that old dam.
That dam he'd fished on for over 65 years.
The cracks in that old dam slowly expanded into larger ones
day after day. Month after month. Year after year.
Red had grown to love that old dam, accustomed
not to the fishing (for he never caught many fish)
but rather he'd grown to love the solitude and peace
that the sound that the water brought
but one day the sound of the water began to change
Yes, an architect could have inspected that old dam
as the town committee had thought …after
the dam had given way
It almost killed him that day
not when the dam actually broke,
but when he made the decision to stop going to that old dam
There was something safe about that familiar place
that familiar sight.
that familiar smell. His familiar spot of that
old dam, but then again he did.
Stay and be swept away or leave and mourn that old dam
a little sooner.
The people in town just new Red would die an old old
man fishing on that old day. But they were wrong.
It all changed for Red when the peculiarity of the water

became predictable. It wasn't just the same for him on that old
dam. He began to question the safety in the familiar.
If he left that old dam and his spot,
he'd have to find something to do with his time. That
frightened Red. In fact, he almost chose to stay on the dam
and be swept away.
But then one day Red did it. He left that old dam,
His place marking the exact spot where the dam would
later break.
It almost did kill him, leaving

That old dam. But one day when the air was cool
and light, and the smell of the freshly cut lawn was sweet,
and an easiness in the day was felt, Red
began to see something that the old dam did not offer him
A chance to live
To experience new things
New sounds
New sights
his spot changed the day he left that old dam
It never ceased to amaze Red when he was out and about
in his new life how many people said it must be
killing him to not be fishing at the dam
but Red would always answer this question by putting
his weathered hands deep within his pockets,
poking around his sparse spare change
While the thought of the old dam breaking
was wreaking havoc on the town, Red would think
to himself, the flood would allow me the chance
of a lifetime. That which he thought would kill him
actually saved his life
And so it was OK when the townspeople laid old Red to rest
In the cemetery under the blooming Bradford pear.
They thought old Red had died of a broken heart.
Oh, if only they knew the truth about his heart...

Giving out because of the fullness of life he was living
but it was OK with Red, because he knew the truth
about that old dam.

(Debbie Vanderslice Shameless, 1998)

Let me end with a quote in scripture by Paul. In Philippians 4:11
b ESV "For I have learned to be content whatever the situation…"
Red was content to just stay and fish on that old dam time and time
again. Year after year. Decade after decade. But something inside
him, in all of us, wanted more. We all want more. It is a God given
desire to want more. No matter how dysfunctional that desire is.
We are all want more. It is just that simple. Is Christ in us enough?
I dare say He is. He is our Contentment. He is our Peace. Our Rock.
Our Salvation. And we are His. His alone. Let's take a chance like
Old Red did. There is a whole life out there waiting for us. Let's
go for it one day at a time. No more. No less. Live in the present
and hope for the future. Let's leave the past in the past.Our time
on earth here is a journey, and until Christ calls us home, we are
therefore on a journey. We may make many mistakes along the way,
but He never gives up on transforming us into what he wants us
to be. We are His, signed, sealed and delivered make no mistake
about it. God will do whatever He must to make us what He wants
us to be. Until that time, We are to live for Him and then we one
day, will see him face to face. O happy day!

Much Afraid

Psalm 56:3

"When I am afraid, I will put my trust in you."

Hinds' Feet on High Places
By Hannah Hurnard
Wikipedia,1955
United Kingdom
Christian Literature Crusade
ISBN 0-86065-192-4

My favorite book is **Hinds Feet on High Places** by **Hannah Hurnard**. It is an old allegorical novel about how God newborn babes in Christ and transforms us into another person goes from crippled believer into a graceful and beautiful believer in Christ.

"It is the story of a young woman named Much Afraid, and her journey away from her Fearing family and into the high places of the Shepard, guided by her two companions, Sorrow and Suffering. It is an allegory of a Christian devotional life from salvation through maturity. It aims to show how a Christian is transformed from unbeliever to immature believer to mature believer, who walks daily with God as easily on the high places of Joy in the spirit as in the daily life of mundane and often humiliating tasks that may cause Christians to lose perspective.

The book takes its title from Habakkuk 3:19 "The Lord God is my strength and He will make my feet like hinds' feet, and he will make me to walk upon mine high places."

The story begins in the Valley of Humiliation with Much Afraid, being beset by the unwanted advances of her cousin, Craven Fear, who wishes to marry her. Much Afraid is ugly from all outward appearances, walking on club feet, sporting gnarled deformed hands, and speaking from a crooked mouth that seems to have been made so by a stroke or the like.

The Good Shepard is tender with Much Afraid, especially in the beginning. However, His many sudden departures may strike the reader as bizarre, given the human penchant to expect kindly souls to never do anything that may be interpreted as ride off as hurtful in any way. Yet, though the Shepard leaves in a moment, He returns the same way at the first furtive cry of the forlorn little protagonist. "Come, Shepard, for I am much afraid!."

"When Much Afraid intimates that she would love to be able to dance upon the high places as do the sure-footed deer, the Shepard commends her for this desire. In order to accomplish this, He offers to plant the seed of love into her heart. At first sight of the long, black Hawthorne-looking seed, she shrieks in fear. So, she relents, and after the initial intense pain, she senses that something is indeed different in her, though she still looks the same, for now." (Wikipedia Christian Literature Crusade)

Can we all relate at some level to Much Afraid? We are all crippled in some way, form, or fashion. It is when we give up and give in to the Savior, that we can then crawl, walk and then run the course the Savior wants us to run. We all have handicaps in life and it is up to Him to change us. What is our role in the sanctification process. Simply put, we sin. Huh, come on Deb, we have to do something? Yes, we sin. In the whole redeeming role, we do nothing except sin. Christ alone saves us. "I found Christ. Was He lost??? No, I was." That is so true and funny. He is the one who saves, not us and all our requirements. Check one, check two, check three. There's that I can mark off my list. Grace cannot be earned or bought by us. It is by faith or grace unseen that we choose God. We can do it every day if we need to. I use to do this every day. I didn't exactly trust Him all the way. So I prayed for Christ to come inside me everyday. Some might have thought "how immature" of you Deb. But I was just a newborn in Christ. I didn't know all the ins and outs of the Christian faith. I knew I needed Christ. Lord knows I needed something in my life. I was sick and tired of being sick and tired.

I call it the restroom revival. Half asleep I stumbled into the bathroom and said, "Come inside me." That was it. No angels appeared. No earthquake. No band of angels singing to me. Nope. Just me and the floor. Or if you need to class that up. I was hugging the toilet because I had downed 8 Bud Lights. Needless to say, I was hungover. Some start to my Christian walk. I "told" God that even though I was such a sinner that from now on till He takes me home, that I would follow Him all the days of my life. It has been a wild ride since I was 17, and God has never left my side. He has been with me all the time. The good, the bad and the ugly. If there is one thing I cannot be without it is the presence of God. I have two personalities. One with Christ and one without Christ. Things go a lot smoother with God, than without Christ. He, God Almighty, transforms us totally when we give our lives to Christ. We are transformed, or changed, so slowly, even painfully, into what God wants us to be. Everything that we go through is never wasted. God will use Satan's game of shame to trip us up or to try and confuse us. But God, in His infinite love and growth loves us too much to leave us stuck in the muck and mire of self- destruction. Even our bad habits and shortcomings are transformed OVER TIME. Life is a journey, not a destination. We must learn the word I hate... PATIENCE. I use to play tennis at a division I school, SMU, and was the most patient player you have ever seen. I would hit 100 balls for a point. Everybody hated to play me because I would stay out there 2-4 hours to win. My opponent would have to hit 35-50 winners in order to win the match. Most girls could not. Thus no one liked to play me. God uses us in all our flaws and like Much Afraid, we are transformed during the journey not by the end result, the destination., but rather we are healed as we are in the journey.

Peace comes not from the destination but rather from the journey. Those of us who have been abused find peace in not the final destination but rather in small steps of the journey. I have run my one and only marathon. I finished without walking at all one step at a time. Although slow and a searing pain in my knee, I had to finish the 26.2 mile race by hopping my way to the finish line.

AA is like that. How does one stay sober? One day at a time and look up, and it is 10 years. I have been sober over 15 years. I was a pill popping addict. Hydrocodone was my drug of choice. How have I stayed sober? I would rather have peace than have the numbing effect of the hydrocodone. Do I ever crave drugs or a high? Without a doubt, yes. The journey is one day at a time. Day after day. It is true for all addicts. We stay clean one day at a time.

Are you disappointed in your author? I am sorry, but I am very human. I can give you all the terrific excuses why I did drugs. I can make a very compelling story of why I needed to numb myself. I was a master manipulator. I knew just how to to obtain pity from virtually any walks of life

But then I set out on a journey. I was tired of excuses that I told myself and others. It was then, when I got totally honest with myself that I began to change. Not all at once, but simply one day at a time. It has been over a decade that I have abused prescription drugs and went doctor shopping. Maybe you can relate or maybe your fix was alcohol, drugs also, and the list goes on and on. We are so good that we could/can talk our way out of anything. We are master manipulators aren't we? We are all on a journey I think. Some of us are born into difficult circumstances. Others are treated like royalty where they are never said "no" to. Whatever cross we must bear, it can either hinder us or spur us on in the this thing called life. We are all on this journey and God brings certain people in our lives to help us. Everyone? Yes, everyone. We can learn from each person that will cross our lives. That may sound hokey I don't mean for it to. But as hokey as it sounds, God doesn't waste anything on us. He can use everything we encounter for us to learn from. God is not into wasting things. Not for a minute. Are things are good? Absolutely not. All things are not good. Sometimes bad things happen to us, but God can use that bad and turn it into good for us. God is into the good business. Genesis 50:20a says, "As for you, you meant evil against me, but God meant it for good..." (ESV)

We can turn anything or situation into good, since God is into that kind of business. Life is a journey not a destination. None of us ever arrive at life. It is only when we cross the finish life that we have arrived...in heaven. Until that day may we all keep running one step at a time. No matter the situation. Or circumstance, or dilemma, or hardship, or death and the list goes on and on

Part 2

THE SOLUTION

Chapter 5

Venturing Out

John 8:32
*"And you will know the truth
and the truth will set you free."*
(ESV)

One thing we need to do as far as overcoming grief is to get outside at least 45 minutes a day. Get real you may be saying," But there is something soothing about the outdoors." I did not do this for over a year after Martha died. It was just scary and overwhelming. But eventually I did get outside. And boy did it make all the difference in the world. I suffer from depression and the way I kept it at bay was playing hours and hours of tennis outside. We had no indoor courts at the time and so I was forced to run or lift weights and also aerobics. Just that alone was enough to keep my depression at bay. Then throw in the tennis and I never had a problem with depression.

When my best friend died, Martha, I became like a hermit. I stopped dead in my tracks. I wouldn't even go to the grocery store. I took my daughter to school and picked her up. Those were the only places I went. To and from her school. I not only closed my heart to places I use to go, I even closed my heart to God. I finally accepted the fact that Martha was not coming back and that she was gone.

Really gone. And so I wrote, wrote, and wrote. There is something soothing and healing about writing. It has such a cathartic feel to it.

Out of bad can good come. Out of great suffering can come peace. And the list just goes on and on.

I felt so broken when my best friend died. Moving on seemed so wrong, but as time went on, my pain began to lessen, but these words remained me of Martha, and the thorn in my side didn't seemed as painful as it once was. As I got outside something really miraculous seemed to happen. I noticed the barren shrubs, the little flowers that seemed to survive the change in weather. Martha died in late November and everything was barren. No life. But as I got outside my depression began to slowly lift and my spirits soared. I even talked to Martha on my long hour walks. Of course I could care less if the neighbors thought I was silly or crazy. I knew Martha could hear my prayers about her family. But there were two people I could not talk to or pray for. One was God and the other was me. I was so angry at Him. I even gave Him the proverbial finger. Not once but every day. Surely Martha could not see all my anger at God. Or could she?

When we venture out for the first time after a loss or tragedy, we are super duper sensitive. Our emotions are raw. When I went out to the grocery store after Martha died, I saw her everywhere or so it seemed. I have never had such a strange things happen. She was in the frozen foods, the meat section. Everywhere I went I thought I saw her. Now after my stroke, my mind played big time tricks on me. It, the stroke and the effects can alter your memory. My short term memory is nill but boy howdy is my long term awesome. So I live with the effects of the stroke. Memory issues are the most prevalent to me. I can remember nothing of the days but months I can rock it. But this is all part of God's refining in my life. I live by faith on a daily basis. It is what it is. I have learned to live with it. It is all part of God's eternal plan. Like a blacksmith that molds his object into what he wants, so too is God's molding me into His creation. Or the potter and his clay, sculping the clay into what he wants. That is called the sanctification process in

God's word.. it does not end until we die. We are a constant work in progress, Here is a poem that I wrote after my best friend and prayer partner, Martha, died. See what you think and can you relate to it.

The Refining
By Debbie Vanderslice
New Hope Publishing, 1998
P. 80

The Refining
Westbow Publishing, 2015
p. 166-167

The Refining

Sometimes this grief washes over me
like the ocean waves crashing against the sand.
Unending. Ceaseless. Perpetual.
To the mere spectator turned vacationer
the water brings with it peace, solitude, and rest.
But to the resident who beaches upon
its shore day after day and month after month,
the waves carry pain, loneliness, and grief.
How long, O Lord
will the waters captivate my life?
My every move, thought, response.
My world stopped while the rest of the world rudely went on
My tears flowed unceasingly
while others seemed to smile effortlessly.
Where is my hope O God
Who is my avenger today O Lord
Why do these lips honestly confess the horrors of my heart
For whatever is gone now
I can rest assured that

You are still in control
and will one day reveal the seemingly painful madness
of the here and now
to the overwhelmingly speechless perfection
of Your divine plan.

Your method is perfect.
Your timing is perfect
Your refining is perfect
May this life of mine not tarry in vain
as I seek Your hand during this molding process

Debbie Vanderslice
Shameless
New Hope Publishers
2008

What then is the solution to obtain peace during difficult times. There is no hard and fast rule to this age old dilemma? I think it is two-fold. One, surround yourself with lots of family and friends, not anyone who dismisses your lose. Supportive people who will hold your hand as you go through the states of grief. I like Kubler-Ross stages of grief. She is right on. And keep in mind we can jump back and forth with the stages.

The second thing is it would be good to do is, be honest. If we need to be alone, then so be it. One is family and two be around honest people. Honesty is the best policy. Especially with grief. Here is a poem I wrote after Martha died. It, writing, was the only place I knew to go.

See what you think of it perhaps you can relate to them.

My Road

I'm venturing down a road, O Lord
That doesn't feel quite familiar
I'm unsure where it's leading
Yet that stops me not.
It is a dangerous steep path
And nothing is familiar, O dear God.
I find myself unable to go back
where predictability was my refuge
Something is beckoning me further on the road,
So addicting in its uncertainty.
Could it be, O sweet Jesus
that what draws me towards the darkness
Is the illumination of You?
For in this blind walk of mine perhaps
I'm finally beginning to see who You are
and whose I really am.

**Shameless, Debbie Vanderslice, .New
Hope Publishers, 2008 p.9**

Sometimes must put on our big boy pants and venture out of our comfort zone. It may be small, such as taking a different way home. Or maybe big such as taking that job in another state. Only you know what to do. It may be strange but you know what is best, and consider getting advice from a trusted person who knows you best. This may be a best friend or relative or even a therapist. It may be unfamiliar to you. That is ok, there can be healing to venture out into the unknown. Change is scary. The unknown is scary stuff. I won't lie. It is quite painful. In every decision we make a choice to either accept or decline. The challenge that is in front of us.

But regardless of the situation in front of us we can grow leaps and bounds. Only God has the master plan. It is through the darkness and pain that we grow. Out of hardships comes success. Out of darkness comes the light. And isn't Christ called The Light? The bright morning star? See if you can relate

To this poem I wrote after Martha died.

Bed of Pain
Isaiah 42:3
Shameless
2008
New Hope Publisher

"My tears have been my food day and night"
Shameless, Debbie Vanderslice 2008
New Hope Publishing (p. 93)

Lay down upon this bed of pain.
The sorrows deep you can't contain.
I come gently to tuck you in
And hold you close from evil's den.
Though your heart is a well dug deep
I'll soften your pillow so you will sleep.
The bliss of peace will overflow
My healing love you will know.
Sleep well with this longing of Mine
For I'm the Bliss you will find.

Brand New

2 Corinthians 5:17b
"The old has passed away; behold the new has come."
(ESV)

When we become Christians, our past, present, and future sins are gone. Nullified. Erased. We are a new person in Christ and we have peace for about an hour. Then Satan enters the picture. Satan is angel too. He loves to get all dressed up as an angel of light. He is the author of confusion. If we can identify Satan as the one who brings up our old sins then we are fighting him in this battle of old us. Remember we fight Satan everyday in the tv, news, schools, and the list can go on and on. If we can identify our weakness then we are half way home. I am not saying to blame everything on Satan like some Christians do, but I am saying to be aware of him.

I am sure that all of us have regrets or have do overs in this life. We all live with regret on perhaps a daily basis. However I have learned something from a wise wise woman. All of our mistakes are a part of us. Everyone except Christ made errors and sinned. Without that fact we would not need Christ. Sometimes we come across an arrogant believer who touts his/her perfection. The only one who was perfect was Jesus Christ. Without our confession of sin we are in denial. Total denial. Those type of believers is in every church there is. They believe they live by the good book and profess their devotion to Jesus. I stand very far away from those types of believers. Lighting may strike them. They are members of the arrogant and prideful sect. they put in a request and out comes the desired request. Much like a coke machine. In goes the dollar and out comes the desire product. This is not God's way at all. They tell everyone that they are cured of cancer, every request you can think of. it turns God into a sugar Daddy. Sometimes He says no to His children. If we try to figure that out, then we are headed down a dark and lonely road.

I had something I like to call the 'restroom revival.' It was sometime in late November. The kind of morning where it was too cold to get out of bed. I remember I sucked it up and went, on the way I said, " come inside me Christ." No bells and whistles. No parting of the back yard, no manna falling from heaven. It was a true confession of Christ. Was I saved. Yes, signed, sealed, and delivered. I had major doubts about being saved. I struggled every day about it. Was it really that easy? It was and is.

If we hang around people of our past, we are doomed to repeat the past and all our mistakes. If we are sixty and still get drunk with high school buddies then we might have a problem. Not just when they get together for reunions. But every night is happy hour at home. I am not saying to not hang out with high school friends but rather to see if you are living in the past or reliving high school every time you get together with high school buddies. Live for the present and future not in the glory days of the past or high school.

When I became a believer there were places I had tennis and school. Tennis was easy, either call them out or in. Keep up with the score. Easy enough. Then there was school. I had a fool proof system with the help of a friend, Sally. The written part in French was easy but I struggled with the oral part. Sally would lift her head up on the right part and so on and so on. Pretty nifty huh. But boy did I flunk the written part. But that changed on early morning. My youth director had been sharing the Gospel every Sunday night. One early morning on the way to the bathroom I did it. Like the

Nike slogan...just do it. I did it. I asked Jesus to come in. I changed. Stopped cheating in school and tennis. I had turned over a new leaf. I was a new creation in Christ. It was the best decision I ever made.

I am not talking about those hokey canned confessions of Christ, but rather from the heart. When I asked Jesus to come inside my heart while using the bathroom, it was sincere. Granted I said it over and over the next year. It was not canned at all. It was straight from my heart to Christ's ear. I was a new creation in Him. Not cheating in school was a direct conviction of my life in him.

When I became a believer I knew things had to change. There were two places that had to change immediately. My tennis and school. Tennis like I said before was easy. Either in or out. Pretty cut and dried. School was harder. Cheating was every where. I even gave up my fool proof French/German oral parts. But something funny happened. I started to make better grades and play better tennis. Go figure huh? I believe with all my heart that a clean conscience prepares the soul for a better life. I still believe that today. Stopping cheating was one big area I changed, other was tennis. My coach was in a car accident/career ending injuries. I was forced to look elsewhere. Enter a good Samaritan for my tennis. He did not charge me a dime and we worked out for almost three hour a day drilling and playing sets. He was a Godsend to me and my family. I felt like I had been reborn again. I even read the Bible every morning. I was ready for the world. Or so I thought. Satan was lurking around the corner. I, like many believers, think the fight over our souls is over. Well, sort of.

Did I struggle? Yes. Was there a desire to take the easy out. Without a doubt. But I had been given a clean slate. Satan's game is all about doubt. No bells or whistles. Just plain old doubt. "Did God really say not to eat of any tree in the Garden?" (Gen. 3:1b ESV) Doubt. See doubt enters the picture since the dawn of time.

Even if we sleep with 200 men, we can still start over. Our society holds grudges. Satan wants to have us think of the past. The King of Kings is all about the future. That is the ticket. Remember we can start over and over. The world does not like this at all. But that is why Christ came. To forgive our sins. No matter what they are. Let's look at His infallible Word below. Revelation 21:5b…"Behold I am making all things new." (ESV) Colossians 3:10 "…and have put on the new self, which is being renewed in knowledge after the image of its creator." (ESV)

God does not say his mercies are good every other week Not even close. He says every day every morning. If we go to Him as an alcoholic every day that is ok with God. Or a drug addict, and the list goes on and on. Yes, we are forgiven if we come to him. Every second, every minute. Satan loves for us to be afraid to go to Him. He revels in the fact we are going to Christ. It doesn't matter how just that we came. No matter how we are dressed. He would rather see a poor dressed lady than a woman in a suit with perfect hair saying, "I am glad I am not her. Pride it is.

Uncomfortable yes, but heaven minded.

Chapter 7

Satan's Game

"...the man and his wife hid themselves from the presence of the Lord God..." (Gen.3:9b ESV)

Doubt. It is the main component of shame. Eve fell for it and has been used by Satan time and time again. Doubt. Such a little thing. Satan used such a little thing to deceive Adam and Eve. Doubt is not a God given talent. No, doubt is of Satan. That is the big tamale. If Satan can get us the doubt God and all His ways he is half way home. It all goes back to the Garden of Eden. The first thing I am going to do when I get to heaven is to slap Eve for the monthly curse bestowed upon all of us females until the golden age of menopause!!!!!!!!!!

When I became a believer I gave up drugs and alcohol. Christ had made me clean and I started hanging out with a different crowd. The nerdy crowd. The academic crowd. Although I was athletic I could float in between the two crowds. The athletic crowd and the nerdy academic crowd.

Since Eve, and alas sinned the first loving sacrifice God had made for him, animal sacrifices, what part did Adam and Eve. Play? Nothing. Zilth, Zero Right on. It was all God, not man. They sinned. That is what we play today. We play a part of nothing. God does it all. It is the salvation experience. We are covered by

Him. He even made coverings for Adam and Eve. For that to take place their must be animal sacrifices. The old way. The new way is Christ. The Lamb of God had to be slain. He was. Once for all, not over and over.

What exactly is Satan's game? Followers? Yes. Breaking all of God's ways? Yes. How does he do it? Just like the way in the Garden of Eden, Satan uses the old adage of doubt. Satan appeals to Eve and Adam via doubt. If they can doubt God then they are half way home. Satan tricks Adam and Eve into thinking God is holding out on them. He is not.

Satan makes the plan look desirable. Eve eats the appleand gives the fruit to Adam to eat. Their eyes are open and they know the difference between good and evil. Satan tricked Eve and Adam. Doubt. Confusion. Disobedience. A moment of confusion. Satan takes the form of a serpent and sweet talks Eve. Then she deceives Adam. The consequence for women is pain during childbirth. Let me tell you this...I am going to slap Eve when I get to heaven. For the monthly curse and childbirth. We definitely reap what we sow. Then and now.

God made coverings for Adam and Eve for coverings. In order to have skin coverings, there must be skin coverings animal sacrifice. An animal must be killed. Sound familiar to you? It should. It is the foreshadowing of Christ on the Cross. It was known since the dawn of time. The foreshadowing of Christ on the Cross. Everything looks to Jesus since the beginning of time. Always have, always will. I am not saying Satan is everywhere. His agents, yes. Before you jump head First into that water, line it up with the Word of God. If it again, again does not support the Bible walk, no run, towards God. He will never lead you astray. Satan is much smarter than to appear in a red suit with horns and smoke coming out of his nostrils.

I love Frank Peretti and his books on spiritual warfare. He hits a homerun in my book. God has the final say. We accept Christ, end of story. Right? Wrong.

When we give our lives to Christ that's it. Done deal. Wrong.

Sure we will struggle with all sorts of addictions and situations. It says in God's Word that sins are carried out to the 4th and 5th generations. Yes, there is a propensity to have a particular sin, such as alcoholism and drug addiction and the list can and does go on and on. We heal by working the program, AA or NA. we can have victory over these things one day at a time. Yes I have had victory one day at a time over drug addiction. Preferably over hydrocodone. I am 10 years sober. No small feat for me. I would not trade those 10 years for anything. My faith has grown leaps and bounds, but I could slip up. I take it one day at a time...plus I have a great support team. They keep me honest during the dark phases and celebrate the victories with them as well. Perhaps we can be like the lilies of the field, bending and swaying to life's game of growing up. The lilies are there during the difficult and hard situations. It is not if we will suffer but when we will suffer.

God is the author of it all. He knows the final outcome. He wins. End of story, end of book. Let's be like the lilies of the field And sway and bend and be flexible in this life of ours. Life will go so much better if we do this. Lilies of the field. Pretty awesome huh? how sweet it is, how sweet it is.

Chapter 8

To Live is Christ

"For to me is to live is Christ, and to die is gain"
Galatians 2:20 (ESV)

I think we are too spoiled here in America. We should all take a trip to Honduras or somewhere in Central America. Then we would see how the other half lives. Dirt poor. Dirt floors. No running water. Latrines for bathrooms. Yes, I say we are pretty lucky. No air conditioners. The list can and does go on and on.

Did you know that 3/4 of the New Testament by Paul was penned in a prison cell. Shackled and no bathroom amenities. Failing eye sight he wrote and wrote until the New Testament was completed. Inspired by God Himself. Paul was practically blind. But he did complete it. We don't go to our heavenly home until it is our time. I believe that more than I can say after my massive stroke. I was dead for two minutes with my stroke. I went through a grey tunnel and popped out into a brightly covered grassy hill. There was my best friend, Martha. We were wearing shin length robes. I said to Martha, you have hair. She replied, "But of course." Then a man with auburn hair and beard told Martha that is was time to go. I piped up that I wanted to go too. She said," it is not your time yet." Then they were gone. Do I believe in the after life? Oh yes. And I also believe in near death experiences. Then the paramedic said, "she's back. We got a heartbeat." It remains my most vivid memory of Martha and my near death experience.

God never asks us to do anything that He doesn't equip us to do. Yes, if God wants us to do something, He will give us the power and gumption to do it. Just think of the 12 disciples. Within 5 years of Christ dying 11 had been murdered and only one, John, died of natural causes. Would those 11 disciples die for a lie? Be tortured for a lie? I think not. I sure wouldn't.

Yet another solution is Christ alone. He is the answer to every problem . Plus His Word. I am not one of those Bible thumpers who thinks Satan is behind every bad thing that happens. Not some but ALL things work together for good. (Romans 8:28b RSV) Out of the most dire situation comes something good. We may have to look for it. It is there. Take it to the bank. It is a done deal. Let me say this a different way...would you die for a lie? Not just bam someone shoots you and you die. But a slow painful death. As cruxification, or stoned to death, or whipped to shreds, or cruxification upside down. 11 of the 12 disciples all died martyr's death. All but John died horrible deaths. John perhaps was spared by ultimately death so he could write some more of the new testament. It is just a theory of mine. He knows our heart. All of it. And they would not die for a lie. And neither would we!!!!!!!! Now that is living. He is alive, I know that now!!!!!!!!!!!!!!! I wish it did not take a near death experience to solidify that fact.. But now I know. Blessed are those who know this to be true!!!!! Paul was a writer of the New Testament as well. He wrote the majority of the New Testament. He faced death on more than one occasion. He was stoned, whipped, beaten, shipwrecked, and imprisoned. All for Christ. He once was so against Christians that he held the coats of those who stoned Stephen to death. Call him a die hard fan against any and all Christians. Then on the way to Damascus, to hurt more believers, he was blinded by Christ and zip zap a doo he talked with Christ and Paul was converted to Christianity. A total conversion experience for him. He now was all about Christ.

Let's be like Paul. Bend and sway like to lilies of the field. They do not worry about when the nourishing rains will come. They will come. They will last the right amount of time. They are durable. They will endure the rains. Come rain or shine the lilies will endure. My parents owned a flower shop for about 15 years. I soon learned that Christmas, and Easter were the big dates, oh also Valentine's day. Lilies were by far the most popular flower at Easter. The Easter lily last for a reason. It bends and sways to the storms. We should take note of this. It is not if our storms would will come but when. The lily last well beyond 2 weeks. You can hardly kill it!!!!!!!!!!!

Will we take heed and learn from the Easter lily? We would be wise to learn from the lily. It is all part of the refining process. He is making and molding us. See if you can relate to this poem.

The Refining

Debbie Vanderslice
Shameless, 1998
p. 80
New Hope Publishing

Sometimes this grief washes over me
Like the ocean waves crashing against the sand.
Unending. Ceaseless.Perpetual.
To the mere spectator turned vacationer
The water brings with it peace, solitude, and rest.
But to the resident who beaches upon
Its shore day after day and month after month,
The waves carry pain, loneliness, and grief.
How long, O Lord,
Will the waters captivate my life?
My every move. Thought. Response.
My world stopped while the world rudely went on.
My tears flowed unceasingly while the others

> seemed to smile effortlessly.
> Where is my hope, O God?
> Who is my avenger today, O Lord?
>
> Why do these lips honestly confess
> the horrors of my heart?
> For whatever is gone now
> I can rest assured that
> You are still in control,
> and will one day reveal the seemingly painful
> madness of
> the here and now,
> to the overwhelmingly speechless perfection
> of your divine plan.
> Your method is perfect.
> Your plan is perfect.
> Your timing is perfect.
> Your refining is perfect.
> May this life of mine not tarry in vain
> as I seek Your hand during this molding process.

So there we are. What do we do during difficult times. We simply bend and sway with the situations like the lily. Like The Word says. If we are type A such as myself, we need to learn to bend more. God is forgiving and flexible. He knows us too well. Better than anyone. He is in control of the madness called our lives. He is our fortress and strength. Our beacon and light. He is the answer to all our prayers. Simply put we are His and He is ours. We can do anything with Him by our side. I hope you liked this book. It was cathartic to write it. I hope you experienced some healing from it.